W9-COJ-878

A FRIEND
SHOULD BE
ATHLETIC,
POETIC,
BUT
MOST OF ALL
MAGNETIC

A FRIEND SHOULD BE
ATHLETIC, POETIC,
BUT MOST OF ALL
MAGNETIC

BILLY SPRAGUE

ILLUSTRATIONS BY DENNAS DAVIS

WOLGEMUTH & HYATT, PUBLISHERS, INC.
BRENTWOOD, TENNESSEE

© 1990 by Billy Sprague. All rights reserved.
Published November 1990. First Edition.
Printed in the United States of America.
97 96 95 94 93 92 91 90   8 7 6 5 4 3 2 1

Illustrations © by Dennas Davis. All rights reserved.

No part of this publication may be reproduced, stored in
a retrieval system, or transmitted in any form by any
means, electronic, mechanical, photocopy, recording, or
otherwise, without the prior written permission of
publisher, except for brief quotations in critical reviews
or articles.

Wolgemuth & Hyatt, Publishers, Inc.
1749 Mallory Lane, Suite 110
Brentwood, Tennessee 37027

for Rose,
who tugs at my heart
from Heaven

A FRIEND
SHOULD BE
ATHLETIC

HE SHOULD
RUN
TO YOUR
DEFENSE

JOG YOUR
COMMON
SENSE

AND
HURDLE
YOUR
DAILY SINS

AND A
FRIEND
SHOULD BE
POETIC

HE SHOULD
PICTURE THE
SHAPE
OF YOUR
SPIRIT

IMAGINE
A WAY
TO BE
NEAR IT

AND
WORD-PAINT
THE TRUTH
SO YOU'LL
HEAR IT

BUT
MOST OF
ALL...

A FRIEND
SHOULD
BE
MAGNETIC

HE SHOULD
ATTRACT
YOUR
ATTENTION

PUSH
AWAY
DOUBT

REPEL
YOUR
PRETENDING

AND
THEN
DRAW YOU
OUT

HE SHOULD
SEND
INVISIBLE
RAYS

WITH
ONLY A
GLANCE

AND TUG
AT YOUR HEART
ACROSS ANY
DISTANCE